AROUND THE WORLD ON

80

HORSES

JILL NEWTON

To Henry, Arlo and their amazing mummy Sarah

First published in 2024 by Child's Play (International) Ltd
Ashworth Road, Bridgemead, Swindon SN5 7YD, UK

Published in USA in 2024 by Child's Play Inc
250 Minot Avenue, Auburn, Maine 04210
US English adaptation by MaryChris Bradley

Distributed in Australia by Child's Play Australia Pty Ltd
Unit 10/20 Narabang Way, Belrose, Sydney, NSW 2085

ISBN 978-1-78628-807-3
IP250624CPL07248073

Printed in Delhi, India

1 3 5 7 9 10 8 6 4 2

A catalog record of this book is available from the British Library

www.childs-play.com

Can you find **80** living breeds in this book?

HORSE
CONTENTS

It's difficult to imagine how different the world would be if humans had not teamed up with the horse.

Armor-clad chargers took knights on crusades; the tough Pony Express mustangs sped across the United States with news of a president's election; and sultans gave their finest stallions to royalty. One horse even had his own TV show!

In this book we will discover some of the incredible journeys made by this amazing animal, and explore the varied landscapes and climates it has inhabited.

Let's find out how horses have helped shape the world we live in today.

PREHISTORIC HORSES

Millions of years ago many different types of prehistoric horses lived in North America, but only one type, the Eohippus (also called the *dawn horse*), survived. This dawn horse eventually developed into *Equus caballus*, the modern horse.

More than 55 million years ago, the warm and humid North American climate became colder and drier. The forests began to shrink, and the buds and berries that the dawn horse ate were disappearing. The shrinking forest made it harder for this primitive horse to hide from predators like the wolf and hyena. Needing to run away, its legs rapidly evolved to become longer and straighter, moving only backwards and forwards. The muscles at the top of the leg became stronger, whereas the muscles below the knee disappeared. Springy tendons developed in their place, working like pogo sticks when the foot hit the ground, saving a lot of energy.

During the Ice Age, almost 36,000 years ago, the sea level between North America and Eurasia (the Bering Strait) fell by more than 328 feet, making it possible for humans and animals to cross from one continent to the other. Many prehistoric horses traveled to Europe, where they survived due to their incredible stamina and ability to adapt. Included in this number was *Equus stenonis*, the ancestor of early horses, zebras, and asses.

When the ice melted, the Bering Strait flooded again, and travel between North America and Eurasia was impossible once more. The horses that remained in North America, such as the New World stilt-legged horse, became extinct over time because of overhunting and changes in climate and vegetation. Now there were no horses in North America at all! It was only later, when human explorers brought them from their own lands, that the horse was once again found in North America.

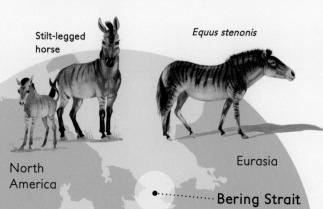

Stilt-legged horse

Equus stenonis

North America

Eurasia

Bering Strait

EOHIPPUS

The prehistoric horse developed a longer neck and jaw so it could graze on the tough plains grass.

EOHIPPUS
(THE DAWN HORSE)

MESOHIPPUS

MERYCHIPPUS

EOCENE	**OLIGOCENE**	**MIOCENE**
56 MILLION YEARS AGO	34 MILLION YEARS AGO	23 MILLION YEARS AGO

FOREST HORSE

A million years ago, the primitive *Equus caballus* lived in the mixed forest-grass areas of mid-Europe, an environment similar to the one it had left behind in North America.

The Latvian horse is a descendant of the forest horse. From here, some horses began to migrate, adapting to new and varying landscapes and climates.

ORIENTAL HORSE

Some horses migrated to hot, dry lands, in the south and east of Europe. These horses became lighter and smaller. They developed long legs and narrow bodies for speed, large nostrils for moistening the dry desert air, and short, fine coats to reflect the sun.

The Iranian Asil (meaning 'pure') is a descendant of the oriental horse

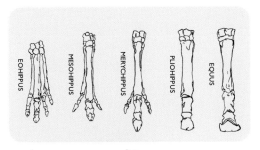

The primitive horse (Merychippus) began to put its weight forward onto the middle of its three front toes, making it even faster. Eventually, this middle toe became one wide toe—the hoof!

PLIOHIPPUS

EQUUS

PLIOCENE	PLEISTOCENE	HOLOCENE
5 MILLION YEARS AGO	2.5 MILLION YEARS AGO	MODERN DAY

DRAFT HORSE

Other horses made their way to Northern Europe and adapted to the wet, marshy environment. They became large and slow moving, with wide, flat hooves, and their coats became wiry and thick to keep out the damp.

The Ardennes is a descendant of the primitive draft horse.

DID YOU KNOW?

The size of its habitat influences the size of the horse, which is why the Shetland, despite being a draft horse, is so tiny!

IBERIAN HORSE

More than 20,000 years ago, during the last ice age, some northern European horses migrated south, settling on the Iberian Peninsula.

These mountain-dwelling horses became incredibly agile, developing deep, broad chests so their lungs could cope with the high altitude.

The Garrano is a descendant of the Iberian horse.

More than 55 million years ago, the horse evolved from a fox-sized creature living in forests into an animal reaching up to 6.5 feet tall, adapted to living on the plains.

Originally, prehistoric horses were found only in North America until the arrival of the Ice Age. This caused the sea level to fall by more than 328 feet, and enabled horses to migrate by land from North America into Siberia. From Siberia, these ancient horses roamed Eurasia, adapting to their new habitats.

DOMESTICATION

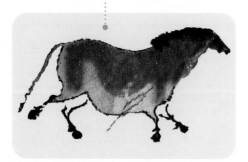

More than five-and-a-half thousand years ago in Kazakhstan, the Botai culture bred horses for their hides, milk and meat. They selectively bred white horses with leopard-spot markings. When the Botai culture died out, the horses became feral and their coats reverted to their natural dun color, blending in with their environment. Przewalski's horse is the only direct descendant of the Botai horse.

During the Late Bronze Age, the Sintashta culture, from the Volga Don region of the Steppes, realized the full potential of the horse. They bred horses with straight, strong backs and calm temperaments. These mainly chestnut-colored horses pulled the newly created spoked-wheel chariots long distances in search of tin, gold and fertile land. By 1500 to 100 BCE this *super* breed had replaced almost all other horse populations across Eurasia.

STONE AGE	BRONZE AGE	CLASSICAL AGE
2 MILLION YEARS AGO	3000 BCE – 1200 BCE	8TH CENTURY BCE – 6TH CENTURY CE

In 1400 BCE, the Hittite Empire built stronger chariots, using newly discovered iron. They also bred stronger horses. The best oriental horses were brought down from the mountains of Turkey and Iran, and completed an intense seven-month program of training on a diet of the finest corn. Large, spirited horses with strong backs were the result. The bony horn-like growths on their heads gave them a slightly ox-headed appearance. These were ambling horses—fast and nimble, capable of jackrabbit starts and sharp spins.

The Ferghana and Nisean horses were the most valued in the ancient world and were descendants of the Hittite horse.

The Phoenicians were the greatest merchant power in the ancient world. By 1100 BCE they had created trading centers along the Mediterranean coast. They traded well-bred, ox-headed horses, along with purple dyed fabric, glass, and cedar, for silver and tin. These horses were bred with native mares from the Celt-held Iberian mountains. Incredibly swift, strong ambling horses were produced. In 600 BCE, the Galician Celts arrived in Ireland in pursuit of tin, bringing their horses with them.

TRAINING

TRADE

Galician horse

Ambling horses perform a four-beat gait, which is a smooth and fast 'running' walk, hence their name. Riders could travel comfortably for long distances and over rough terrain long before the stirrup was invented. This kind of journey would have been incredibly painful on a trotting horse! Ambling horses were extremely valuable in the Middle Ages. The jennet was popular with Spanish nobility, while Henry VIII brought the Irish Hobby over to England for his personal racing stables.

CROSSBREEDING

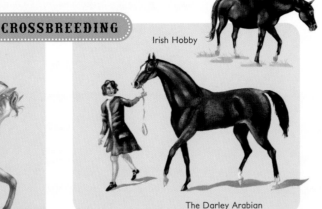

Irish Hobby

The Darley Arabian

Beginning in the 17th century, stallions—mainly the Darley Arabian—were crossed with the Irish Hobby and native English mares, to create the Thoroughbred.

MIDDLE AGES
476CE – 1453

EARLY MODERN
1500 – 1800

As roads improved in the 18th century, larger, stronger horses were needed to pull carriages, while galloping breeds were developed for racing and light cavalry. All these horses tended to be trotters, so the need for ambling horses in Europe declined. The jennet and the Hobby do live on today through breeds like the Connemara, Peruvian Paso, the Tennessee Walking Horse, and of course, the Thoroughbred, the fastest horse in the modern world!

The jennet was crossed with oriental horses from North Africa, creating the nimble Barb. When the Barb was crossed back with the jennet, the athletic Andalusian was created.

Early humans domesticated, bred, and trained these primitive horses, though at separate times, in different places, and by using various techniques. Humans transported the best stallions across the seas to new lands. These stallions were crossbred with native mares, creating powerful workhorses, bold battle mounts, and swift steeds, spreading trade across many countries.

There are more than 350 breeds of horses and ponies today. Not one of these breeds is wild; and each has been bred by humans for different purposes.

The onager is the rarest of the living horse relatives. Poaching and disease have caused onager numbers to fall rapidly. However, some zoos have a successful breeding program. The onager catapult was a medieval weapon with a sling said to equal the force of a kick from an onager.

A hinny is a cross between a stallion (a male horse) and a jenny (a female donkey). It has the looks and strength of its father but is slower and more careful like its mother. Although the hinny takes its time, it can keep going for much longer than the mule.

ONAGER

HINNY

The tapir has been around for more than 20 million years and has changed very little in appearance. Young tapirs are called calves. They have striped and spotted coats—similar to the markings of the prehistoric dawn horse—that help camouflage them in the forest.

TAPIR

RHINO

MULE

A mule is a cross between a jack (a male donkey) and a mare (a female horse). They live longer and are hardier than the horse, and less willful than their donkey dad!

Energetic, agile and bold, mules were the mount of choice for medieval aristocracy. Cosimo de' Medici favored a brown mule, while Cardinal Wolsey rode on a white mule.

When Marco Polo first set eyes on a rhinoceros in 14th century Africa, he thought he'd discovered a unicorn. He spread the word that rather than being a beautiful white horse that could only be tamed by maidens, the unicorn resembled an elephant and enjoyed wallowing in mud!

ZEBRA

A horse escapes danger by bolting in a straight line, but its cousin the zebra takes a zig-zagging path. The zebra's black and white stripes confuse biting flies, making it difficult for them to land.

DONKEY

Donkeys are clever and curious, nimble and sociable, but they are not stubborn, despite their reputation. They have a strong sense of self-preservation and prefer to do what is best for donkey, which is not always best for the human! A donkey's big ears not only hear another's bray from up to 60 miles away, they also work as a fan to keep the donkey cool!

ZONKEY

A zonkey is the offspring of a male donkey and a female zebra. Like the mule and the hinny, this crossbreed is almost always infertile, so they are rarely born in the wild. Zonkeys can run at speeds of up to 37 miles per hour!

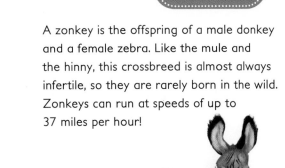

QUAGGA

The quagga, a close relative of the plains zebra, was driven to extinction by over-hunting in the 19th century. Happily, the decoding of its DNA combined with a program of selective breeding means that the quagga is once more alive and kicking in South Africa.

SEAHORSES

The ancient Greeks thought these beautiful creatures were baby *hippocampi*, the tailed horses of the sea god Poseidon. It's easy to see why!

The horse family tree is fairly small, but it includes some interesting members. Horses belong to an order named Perissodactyla, or *odd-toed ungulates*. Their middle toe bears their weight forward, allowing them to run efficiently.

They are large animals with a long lifespan, living up to 50 years. Odd-toed ungulates are *hind-gut fermenters*, which means they digest food in their very long intestines. Horses' intestines can be up to 85 feet long! This allows them to run immediately after eating. The cow, a member of Artiodactyla, or *even-toed ungulates*, by contrast, has four stomachs and needs a good nap after lunch!

Something else that holds this oddly matched family together: they all have elongated heads with a long upper jaw, allowing them to graze easily.

9

A horse's height is measured in *hands* from the heel to the withers. One hand equals four inches. A Belgian Draft named Big Jake was one of the tallest horses in the world, measuring a massive 20.3 hands. That's a 6.8 foot climb!

Horses love grazing but cut grass can kill them. Grass cuttings release gas and horses cannot burp or vomit, so the grass will make their stomach swell and give them a bad stomachache called *colic*. A horse with colic needs immediate care, or it could die.

Horses come in lots of different colors but are rarely born white. Instead, gray horses' hair becomes lighter with age, like us!

Horses are literally big-hearted. Their hearts are nearly 10 times larger than ours!

The tail is more than a fly swatter, it is also a great mood detector! The horse will carry it high to attract attention, while a swishing tail shows that the horse is agitated or confused. A horse that is scared, ill or feeling inferior will have its tail between its legs.

DID YOU KNOW?

A baby horse is called a foal, and it can see and walk as soon as it's born! A young female horse is a filly and a young male horse is a colt.

Some horses have white markings on their legs above the fetlock and below the knee, which are called *socks*. White markings on a horse's face are called stars, stripes, snips, or blazes.

Tail

Dock

Pelvis

Patella

Hock

Fetlock

Pastern

Coronet

Star Stripe Snip Blaze White face

Hooves are made from keratin. This is the same substance as our hair and nails. The *frog* is a triangular shaped pad on the underside of the foot. It acts as a shock absorber and is also a scent gland. Horses can track each other by sniffing the ground!

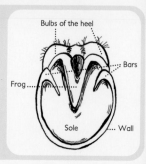

Bulbs of the heel

Bars

Frog

Sole

Wall

The mane protects their neck from rain.

Poll

Ear

Mane

Withers

20.3hh

Shoulder

Elbow

Knee

Heel   Chestnut

There are 10 muscles in a horse's ear (we only have three), enabling them to rotate 180 degrees. The fluffy hair protects the inner ear from bugs, grass, and the weather.

Eye

Horses have the largest eyes of all land mammals. Their eyes are on the sides of their head, giving them 350-degree vision, so they can easily spot any predators.

Nose

Horses cannot breathe through their mouth.

A horse's sense of smell is 500 times sharper than a human's, and almost as keen as a scent hound's! This helps it determine if something is edible or poisonous.

Whiskers

Horses have two blind spots—one directly behind them and the other in front of their face. Whiskers are essential for judging distance between objects and detecting sounds, sending warning signals that travel 249 miles per hour to the brain!

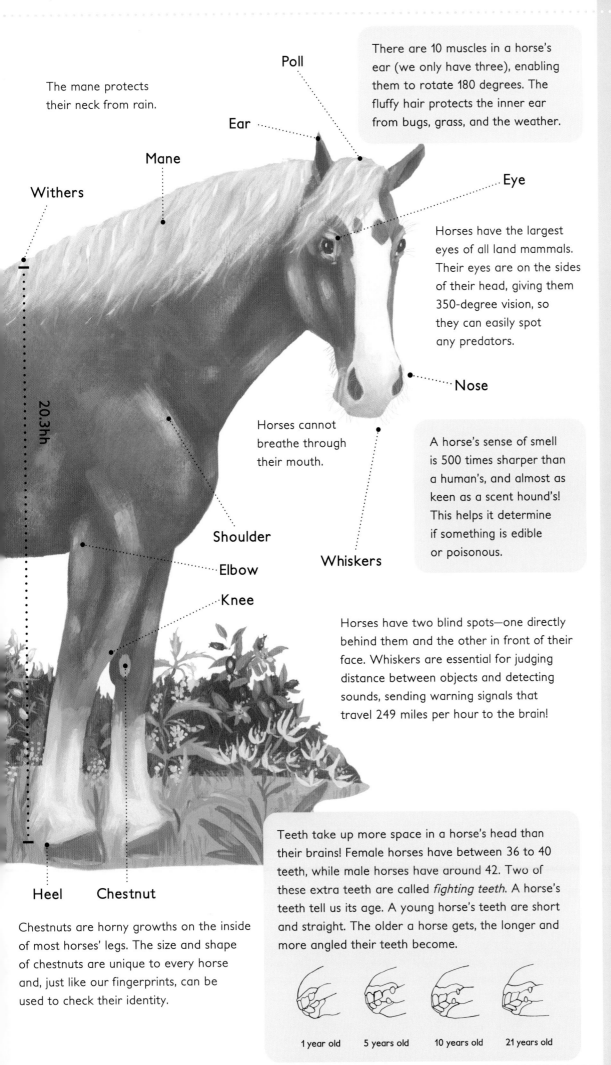

Horses are happiest outside, spending a lot of time grazing. They are known as *trickle feeders*. They eat little and often as their stomachs cannot cope with large amounts of food at once.

Did you know horses can sleep standing up? Their legs lock in a way that disengages the muscles, so the leg bones prop them up while dozing. This enables them to flee immediately should any danger arise.

Horses do not have collar bones. Their front legs are attached to the spine by a strong band of muscles, tendons, and ligaments, enabling their legs to stretch out and cover more ground at speed.

Chestnuts are horny growths on the inside of most horses' legs. The size and shape of chestnuts are unique to every horse and, just like our fingerprints, can be used to check their identity.

Teeth take up more space in a horse's head than their brains! Female horses have between 36 to 40 teeth, while male horses have around 42. Two of these extra teeth are called *fighting teeth*. A horse's teeth tell us its age. A young horse's teeth are short and straight. The older a horse gets, the longer and more angled their teeth become.

1 year old   5 years old   10 years old   21 years old

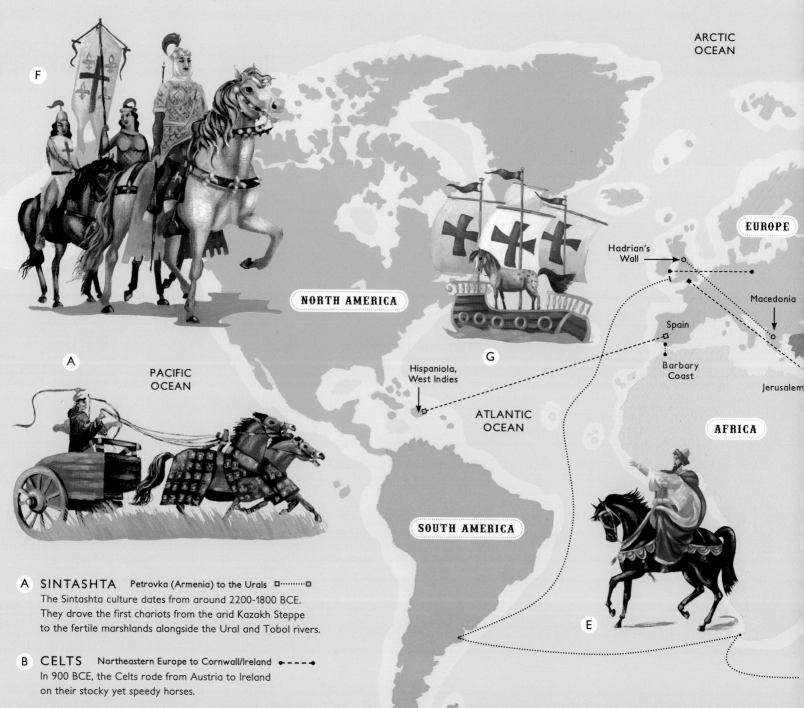

ARCTIC
OCEAN

EUROPE

Hadrian's
Wall

Macedonia

Spain

NORTH AMERICA

Barbary
Coast

Hispaniola,
West Indies

Jerusalem

ATLANTIC
OCEAN

AFRICA

PACIFIC
OCEAN

SOUTH AMERICA

SOUTHERN
OCEAN

A **SINTASHTA**   Petrovka (Armenia) to the Urals   □┄┄┄┄□
The Sintashta culture dates from around 2200-1800 BCE.
They drove the first chariots from the arid Kazakh Steppe
to the fertile marshlands alongside the Ural and Tobol rivers.

B **CELTS**   Northeastern Europe to Cornwall/Ireland   ●┄┄┄┄►
In 900 BCE, the Celts rode from Austria to Ireland
on their stocky yet speedy horses.

C **SILK ROAD**   Ferghana Valley to Jicheng (Beijing)   ■┄┄┄┄■
In 138 BCE, Zhang Qian of the Chinese Han Dynasty began
to trade silk for the *heavenly horses* from the Ferghana Valleys
in Persia. These beautiful, smooth gaited horses were hugely
popular with the cavalry and ladies of the court.

D **SARMATIANS**   Macedonia to Hadrian's Wall   ○┄┄┄┄○
In 175 CE, Roman Emperor Marcus Aurelius sent 5,500 Sarmatian
warriors to Britain. The Sarmatian female warriors were called
Amazons. The Sarmatians were incredible horse riders, riding hardy,
handsome Kabardian horses. The Sarmatian women, men,
and horses settled in Britain after the Roman Empire collapsed.

E **MOORS**   Barbary Coast to Gibraltar   ●┄┄┄┄●
In 711 CE, the Moors crossed the Strait of Gibraltar to the Iberian
Peninsula. They brought guitars, books, oranges, astronomy, and
horses—the quick, sharp Barb, which was bred with native
Iberian horses.

F **CRUSADES**   England to Jerusalem   ■┄┄┄┄■
In 1147, Queen Eleanor joined the Second Crusade, riding at the head
of her troops, which included some of her ladies-in-waiting on their destriers.

G **COLUMBUS**   Spain to Hispaniola   □┄┄┄┄□
In 1493, Christopher Columbus arrived on the island of Hispaniola
in the West Indies, bringing smooth-gaited Spanish jennets with him.
The conquistadors followed, arriving in 1519, returning the breed back
to North America after its extremely long absence.

H **FIRST FLEET**   UK to Botany Bay   I┄┄┄┄I
In 1788, the First Fleet, made up of 11 ships carrying prisoners from England,
arrived in Australia's Botany Bay. Only seven horses survived the three-month
sea journey, however, and safe arrival wasn't the end of their troubles—now
the horses had to learn to survive in the tough new terrain.

Urals

Petrovka
(Armenia)

Ferghana
Valley

Jicheng
(Beijing)

ASIA

DID YOU KNOW?

A Sarmatian tribe called the lazyges made armor out of horse hoof trimmings, which they shaped into scales.

C

B

D

OCEANIA

INDIAN
OCEAN

Botany
Bay

H

Horse breeds rarely had names before the Middle Ages. Instead, humans chose the type of horse they needed. For instance, the destrier was a strong, spirited European horse just right for a knight in the Middle Ages, and the jennet was an elegant, smooth-gaited horse, ideal for an aristocrat.

Breeding developed as humans tried to create specific horses for specific jobs. Breeds were often named after the places near where they were born.

Let's travel around the world to meet some of these breeds, such as the leaping Lipizzaner, the crag-climbing Peruvian Paso, and the flamboyant festival ponies of the Indonesian islands.

1 IRISH DRAFT

The Irish Draft has an easy-going temperament and is an excellent all-rounder. There is a well-known saying: 'The Irish Draft could plough, sow, reap and mow, go to church and hunt.'

2 CONNEMARA

In 1588, the Spanish Armada ran aground in Galway, where their athletic Andalusian horses escaped to the mountains. They bred with the sure-footed Nordic ponies left by the Vikings, creating the Connemara, a beautiful, versatile pony that jumps like a stag.

3 WELSH MOUNTAIN PONY

Ponies existed on the Welsh mountains long before the Romans arrived. There are four types: Section A, B, C, and section D, known as the Welsh Cob. The smallest, and most spirited, is called the Section A. Despite its fine appearance, it is strong enough to carry a farmer over the mountains, and tough enough to work in the pits.

4 SHETLAND

The tiny Shetland is the strongest breed in existence for its size, able to pull more than twice its own weight. The Shetland's large nostrils warm up the freezing North Sea air before it reaches the pony's lungs.

5 HIGHLAND

The Highland helps people on small farms, works on royal estates, and provides transport during deer hunts. The Garron, a larger type of Highland pony, lives on the mainland and is calm and reliable.

6 DALES

The Dales pony is famous for its fast trot and strong will, and can maintain a speed of 20 miles per hour for long distances without tiring, even when transporting ore from inland lead mines to the coast along rugged roads.

7 FELL

As well as being a royal mount, the Fell pony also helped the Romans build Hadrian's Wall, so you can see the truth in the saying: "You cannot put a Fell pony to the wrong job."

8 EXMOOR

This pony was recorded as living on Exmoor in the Domesday Book. The Exmoor has special features that help it survive the harsh climate: *toad eyes* (hooded eyes), an *ice tail* (to direct water away from its belly) and two coats.

9 CLEVELAND BAY

The Cleveland Bay was once called the *Chapman Horse* (chapmen were early traveling salesmen) and has bluish hooves. It is England's oldest horse breed, bred by monks in the Northern monasteries from the horses brought over by the Sarmatians.

10 NEW FOREST

The New Forest pony roams Hampshire's common lands and roads. It is strong, easy to train, and happy to share the terrain with both walkers and drivers, making it a very safe ride.

11 SHIRE

The Shire was bred by Henry VIII to be the perfect warhorse. Later it worked on farms and pulled trams in towns. Today the Shire is as rare as the giant panda. It is now being used on some farms as part of a conservation program

6 14-14.2hh

2 13-15hh

4 7.9-10.5hh

4

12 16-18hh

3 10.2-12hh

5

12

9

7 6

2

1

UNITED KINGDOM

3

11

13

15

IRELAND

8

14

10

1 15.2-16.3hh

9 15.2-16hh

The Uffington White Horse was carved into the chalk hills during the Bronze Age. It is believed to represent the Celtic horse goddess, Epona.

12-14.2hh 10

13-14.2hh 5

11.1-12.2hh 14

11.3-12.3hh 8

DID YOU KNOW?

Hobby in Gaelic comes from *obann*, meaning swift. Now extinct, the Irish Hobby was a nippy and gaited Gallic warhorse. Hobby mares were bred with Arabian stallions to create the Thoroughbred. Now, a 'hobby horse' is a toy horse for children to ride.

15.2-16hh 15

13 15-17hh

11 16.2-18.2hh

7 13-14hh

For thousands of years different cultures have sailed across the rough waters of the Atlantic and North Sea to the British Isles. Whether they came to trade, invade, or settle, they all brought their own horses.

The UK has more native breeds of horses and ponies than any other country in the world. From the tough and tiny Shetland to the elegant Cleveland Bay, these horses are capable of a wide variety of jobs.

Some of the world's best racehorses have come from Ireland. Its wet, mild climate produces lush, calcium-rich grass, which helps the young horses develop strong, healthy bones.

12 CLYDESDALE

The Clydesdale is the ideal lead horse for a parade. It has a long, high-crested neck, with elegant, feathered legs, and a high-stepping action.

13 THOROUGHBRED

Despite its highly-strung reputation, this agile horse's abilities extend further than racing. Many Thoroughbreds go on to make excellent event horses, show jumpers, and even film stars!

14 DARTMOOR

Kind and sensible, the Dartmoor pony is the smaller neighbor of the Exmoor and was used to transport prisoners across the moors.

15 SUFFOLK PUNCH

Always chestnut and with no white markings, this charming, heavy horse works hard well into its twenties. It's no surprise that a brand of lawnmower has been named after it!

1 ICELANDIC

The pony-sized Icelandic is one of the purest horse breeds, since no other horses are allowed onto the island. Its unique gait, called the *tölt*, enables it to cover rough ground effortlessly and quickly.

2 NORWEGIAN FJORD

The Fjord is a hard-working, friendly pony that pulls carts up the steep, icy tracks that tractors cannot manage. An ancient breed, it resembles the horses in cave paintings, with its thick, upright, two-tone mane, which is commonly roached.

3 BLACK FOREST HORSE

This gentle horse, with its striking dark sorrel coat and flaxen mane, once pulled logs up the Black Forest's steep mountains. Every three years, the town of St Märgen in Germany holds Rossfest, an event that celebrates this stunning rare breed.

4 FRIESIAN

Reliable, handsome, and cheerful, the Friesian is always black and was once the choice of medieval knights. Now the Friesian is popular with television and film casting directors due to its remarkable patience, along with its beautiful long, silky mane, tail, and feathers.

5 HANOVERIAN

The elegant and stylish Hanoverian was originally bred to pull carriages. It is now rated as a world-class competition horse.

6 LIPIZZANER

The Lipizzaner is a truly royal horse. It was bred from the Spanish horse that Emperor Maximillian II so admired. Since 1735, the Spanish Riding School has been based in Vienna, where Lipizzaners are, to this day, trained in *haute école* (French for high school). Pictured here is the *capriole*, a move originally performed on the battlefield to attack the enemy.

7 TRAKEHNER

The Trakehner is one of the oldest warmblood breeds, with just the right balance of Thoroughbred speed and draft horse common sense to help it clear a cross country course quickly.

ICELAND

13hh

1

DID YOU KNOW?
In the 9th century, the Vikings took their horses to Iceland, sailing in open boats across the rough Atlantic Sea. It's no wonder Icelandic horses are considered some of the hardiest in the world.

14.2-15.3hh

4

15.2-16hh

3

15.3-17.2hh

5

13.2-15hh

2

NORWAY

15.2-17hh

7

2

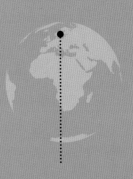

The Vikings and the Celts both rode small, stocky horses across northern European territories. These horses were gaited and comfortable to ride. As weapons and carriages became bigger, larger horses were needed.

The warmblood horse was originally bred in early medieval times when the heavy, native marsh horse was crossed with agile Spanish and oriental horses. There are now a number of warmblood breeds, often named after the area where they are bred.

Modern warmbloods make terrific competition horses, excelling at dressage and show jumping.

NETHERLANDS

7

POLAND

5

15-16.1hh

4

6

GERMANY

3

6

AUSTRIA

FRANCE

SPAIN

PORTUGAL

13-14hh

15.1-16hh

15-16hh

15.2-16.2hh

14-14.2hh

DID YOU KNOW?
The Royal Horses of Cordoba in Spain perform flamenco steps in time to the music of the Spanish guitar.

1 LUSITANO

Hailing from Portugal, the Lusitano is a close relation of the Andalusian. It is strong, with lots of stamina and a great will to learn. This makes it exceptionally good at dressage, where it has won several Olympic gold medals.

2 SORRAIA

Hidden away in the remote Portuguese lowlands, this primitive horse was discovered by a scientist on a hunting trip in 1920. The Sorraia is a direct descendant of prehistoric horses and ancestor of the Lusitano.

3 ANDALUSIAN

The Andalusian's official name is *Pura Raza Española* (Spanish purebred). It is unnervingly intelligent, docile and quick to learn. Its flexible joints allow it to make complicated moves, such as leaps, air kicks, and slow, graceful prances.

4 ASTURCÓN

The small and predominantly black Asturcón has a smooth and comfortable gait. It was such a highly prized mount that it was taken to Ireland to create the hobby horse.

5 BRETON

Docile and kind, the Breton is a useful and strong horse, often seen working in French vineyards and on farms.

15-18hh · **7**

8

ITALY

8 13-15hh

9

11.2-12.2hh · **4**

14-15hh

9

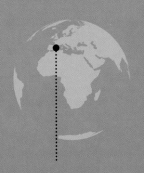

Heavy horses have been important to French life throughout centuries of farming and warfare. There are even prehistoric paintings of primitive horses on the walls of the Lascaux Cave in the South of France.

More than 25,000 years ago, Iberian horses roamed the plains of Portugal and Spain. They are one of the most ancient types of domesticated horse and are ancestors of the modern Andalusian.

All purebred Andalusian horses can trace their ancestry back to a group of horses from a monastery in Cartuja, Spain, where they were initially bred in the 15th century.

6 CAMARGUE

The Camargue is an ancient breed. It's thought it may be a descendant of the identically sized prehistoric horse whose bones were found near the salt marshes of the Rhône river delta, where Camargue horses still run free.

7 PERCHERON

The majestic Percheron has agility, poise, and power. In medieval times it carried knights wearing heavy armor into battle. Today the Percheron is one of the horses used by police forces around the world.

8 HAFLINGER

These kind, long-lived mountain ponies can be traced back to a single stallion. Known as *the horse with the golden heart*, the Haflinger has a nature as beautiful as its appearance.

9 MAREMMANO

This ancient breed has lived in the Tuscan region of Italy since Roman times, when it was believed to be the chosen mount of emperors, such as Marcus Aurelius.

1 PASO FINO

Los Caballos de Paso Fino means horses with a fine step. This little horse is prized in Colombia for its spirit and smooth, fox-trotting action.

2 MANGALARGA MARCHADOR

The National Horse of Brazil is lively but docile and has remarkable stamina. It holds the Endurance record in the Guinness Book of World Records for a ride of 8,694 miles over one-and-a-half years. Good thing it's a very comfortable ride!

3 PERUVIAN PASO

Tough and cheerful with exceptionally long legs, the Peruvian Paso (*paso* means step) travels easily over the craggy mountains.

4 ARGENTINE CRIOLLO

Running through the pampas grass of South America, the hardy Criollo ponies developed powerful lungs. Criollo have a very slow metabolism and can travel for days, and sometimes even weeks, with very little food.

5 ARGENTINE POLO PONY

The Argentinians bred the Criollo with the Thoroughbred for speed and height, making them some of the best polo ponies in the world.

6 FALABELLA

The Falabella is a mix of Criollo, Shetland, Welsh Pony, and the small Thoroughbred. This intelligent and trainable miniature horse (called a horse rather than a pony due to its proportions) makes a great companion, guide, and therapy animal.

7 CHILEAN

The oldest registered breed in South America, this courageous rodeo horse has been working with cows since its ancestors arrived from Spain. Rodeo is the national sport in Chile. Cowhands travel hundreds of miles to compete in these thrilling events. The rodeo in Chile is different from those in the US.

COLOMBIA

BRAZIL

14-15hh

PERU

CHILE

ARGENTINA

13-14hh

1

13-15.2hh

2

14-15.2hh

5

14.2-16hh

2

14-15hh

4

In 1493, explorers from the Spanish and Portuguese empires arrived, with their Iberian horses, on the island of Hispaniola. Many of their horses were left behind as they colonized the Caribbean Islands. Abandoned, the horses adapted to the craggy mountains, high altitudes, sparse food, and harsh limate.

These horses all shared common traits: they were hardy, intelligent, good-natured, and sensible.

DID YOU KNOW?

Huaso (which means cowboy) was spotted jumping over a 6.6 foot high wall to escape from his field. In 1949, Huaso went on to break the world record, by clearing a jump of 8ft, 1in with his trainer Captain Alberto Larraguibel Morales.

6

6-8.5hh

21

1 CANADIAN

In 1665, Louis XIV of France shipped two of his best stallions and 20 mares to Canada. These are the ancestors of the Canadian horse. Energetic, bold and intelligent, it has been said that the mind of the Canadian horse is its strength.

2 MUSTANG

The Mustang is a symbol of the American Wild West. It was once domesticated, but now runs free as a feral horse. Once tamed, it makes a great, sure-footed trail horse.

3 MORAB

With its mix of Morgan and Arab blood, the Morab has amazing stamina, making it a champion endurance horse.

4 MISSOURI FOX TROTTER

Often called the cowboy's Cadillac, the Fox Trotter appears to walk with its front legs, while its hind legs do a sliding trot at a gentle speed of 5-8 miles per hour. This comfortable, steady gait made it a favorite with settlers, like sheriffs and doctors, who needed to travel long distances.

5 QUARTER HORSE

The Quarter Horse, or Cutting Horse, is the oldest of the US breeds and was originally bred to race a quarter mile. Intelligent and sensible, this horse is a star on cattle ranches.

6 APPALOOSA

The Appaloosa is best known for its wonderful spotted coat. They sometimes have striped hooves as well. It was first bred near the Palouse River by the Nez Perce tribe, and is now the official horse of Idaho. Appaloosas have many kinds of markings, including raindrop, blanket, spotted blanket and snowflake.

7 TENNESSEE WALKING HORSE

The Tennessee Walking Horse has a unique four-beat gait—a running walk—thought to be one of the most comfortable rides in the world.

8 MORGAN

Named after its breeder and owner, composer Justin Morgan, this horse can do almost any job—hauling logs one day, winning a harness race the next.

9 CHINCOTEAGUE

Legend says that the original Chincoteague ponies were passengers on a Spanish galleon, which sank off the Virginia coast. The ponies swam to safety on Assateague Island, where their descendants still live today. Every year, the Saltwater Cowboys take part in the Chincoteague Pony Swim from Assateague Island to Chincoteague Island.

14-16hh
1

14-15hh
2

3
14.1-15.2hh

CANADA

DID YOU KNOW?

Fossils found at the Hagerman Fossil Beds in Idaho date back 3.5 million years. Named the Hagerman horse (*Equus simplicidens*), these bones are the oldest remains of the genus Equus discovered anywhere in the world. The Hagerman horse is also the state fossil of Idaho!

6   2

UNITED STATES

4
14-16hh

3

5

14-16hh   5

6

14-16hh

7

14.3-17hh

1

8

14.1-15.2hh

8

9

12-13hh

9

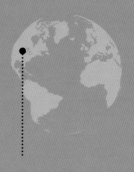

The prehistoric horses that once roamed the forests of North America died out here more than 10,000 years ago.

When horses finally returned to their homeland they were first adopted by the Comanche tribe who became legendary horse riders.

North America is now home to many breeds. There are more horses here than anywhere else in the world—approximately 7.2 million!
A whopping 10 per cent of these horses live in Texas, which has the highest horse population per state.

23

 BASHKIR

High up in the Ural Mountains lives the tough Bashkir. Its curly coat is woven into a cloth, which can be worn by people who are allergic to other fabrics. Fermented Bashkir mare's milk, *kumis*, is still a popular drink in this region.

 ORLOV TROTTER

Russia's most famous breed pulls a *troika* or sleigh across the frozen land. The two outside horses canter, while the single inner horse trots.

 DON

In the past, the Don, known for its endurance, was the mount of the Cossacks. Today, it performs at the International Dzhigitovka Shows where horse and rider display their remarkable skills.

4 YAKUTIAN

The Yakutian's 6in long coat keeps it warm, even when temperatures plunge as low as -76 degrees Fahrenheit.

5 KABARDIAN

This incredible horse is bred more than 2,500 feet above sea level! The Kabardian has an uncanny ability to find its way home, even when cantering down steep, stony roads through the mist and darkness. This is why it is called the King of the Mountain.

6 PRZEWALSKI'S HORSE

The Przewalski's horse (*Equus ferus*, meaning wild horse), pronounced *ji-vaal-ski*, was discovered in this area in the 1960s. Przewalski's horse has two extra chromosomes, so it is only a cousin of the modern horse, though it is a direct descendant of the first domesticated horse, the Botai.

7 MONGOLIAN

The Mongolian horse (which is actually a pony) lives with its nomadic owners and can go long periods without food or shelter. Its tough tail hair is used for bowstrings for violins. The Mongol Derby is the longest horse race in the world, where local semi-feral horses are ridden across the 621 mile route taken by Genghis Khan's messengers in 1224. The prize? Just finishing!

2 15.2-17hh

1 13.1-14hh

RUSSIA

7 12-14hh

MONGOLIA

6 12-14hh

DID YOU KNOW?

There are more horses than people in Mongolia, where there is a saying: "A Mongol without a horse is like a bird without wings."

15.1-15.3hh

3

DID YOU KNOW?

The tough Mongolian horses made excellent mounts for warriors, enabling the fearsome Genghis Khan to conquer the world. This demanding emperor also relied on his horses to provide him with food, drink, entertainment, sport, spiritual power, and a mount to ride in his afterlife.

4

13.1-13.3hh

4

14.1-15.1hh

5

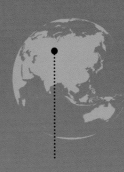

The hardy riding horses, elegant trotters, hardworking pack ponies, and powerful farm horses from this part of Asia all have traits in common. They are tough, undemanding, and obedient.

They must also cope with freezing temperatures, harsh, rocky terrain, and wolves.

Many horses are still essential to everyday life in the remote regions of this land. They are not just working beasts, they are considered a cherished part of the family.

14.2-15.2hh

1

DID YOU KNOW?

This is the seal of Darius I, which shows him using Caspian horses to pull his hunting chariot. It dates from around the 6th century BCE.

9-11.2hh

3

LIBYA

DID YOU KNOW?

Ramses II ruled Egypt more than 3,000 years ago. His stable block, the oldest in the world, was discovered in 1999. It has room for more than 450 horses and is the size of a small village!

EGYPT

1

14.1-15.1hh

2

1 BARB

The Barb, from the Barbary Coast of North Africa, is hardy and fast. It has strong and well-developed hindquarters, making it nimble and able to change direction quickly. The Barb arrived in Spain in the early 8th century. It was bred with native Spanish horses to create the stunning Andalusian.

2 ARABIAN

The beautiful Arabian has had a huge influence on many other breeds. It is easily recognized by its *dished* face and large eyes. They have a high tail carriage, due to having two fewer ribs and one less vertebra. The Arabian holds its head up high, thus gaining its nickname *Drinker of the Wind*.

3 CASPIAN

This ancient horse was barely known outside a small area near the Caspian Sea until 1965. The Caspian looks like a tiny Arabian, but it has been around for thousands of years longer. Despite its size, it steps out like a horse and jumps like a stag!

4 DARESHURI

Bred on the green pastures of the Zagros mountains, the Dareshuri is the direct descendant of the *super horse of the ancient world*, the Nisean. The Qashqai nomads saved this horse from near extinction by careful breeding.

5 AKHAL-TEKE

Elegant and proud, the Akhal-Teke (pronounced *ah-Khal Teh-keh*) appears on the Turkmenistan state emblem, bank notes, and stamps. Famous for making a 235 mile, three-day journey across the desert, without water, this horse is also known for its grace and loyalty. The hairs on the Akhal-Teke's coat are hollow, giving off a metallic sheen, which reflects the sun.

The Akhal-Teke on the Turkmenistan president's coat of arms

TURKMENISTAN

5

IRAN

3

4

15-16hh

4

SAUDI ARABIA

14.2-16hh

5

YEMEN

2

Horses have been ridden across the Arabian Desert since 3,500 BCE. Strong sun and sparse foliage means that oriental breeds possess incredible stamina and speed, making them excellent endurance horses. These spirited and loyal, hot-blooded horses can survive on little water and much less food than most breeds.

Oriental horses have had a huge influence on the development of breeds like the Thoroughbred.

27

1 SPITI

The Spiti is sure-footed and tough, making it a great mountain packhorse.

2 MARWARI

The Marwari horse was used to fight sword-wielding enemies on elephants. The Rajputs placed false trunks on their horses to make them look like baby elephants. The enemy elephants retreated, refusing to attack the fake baby elephants.

3 KATHIAWARI

Bred in the royal palaces of India, the Kathiawari is very loyal, brave, and alert. It has a *revaal* gait, allowing it to travel quickly over long distances without tiring. Sometimes, they are born with one blue and one brown eye, which is considered bad luck.

4 MANIPURI

The fearless Manipuri pony was considered sacred and was never used as a work animal. The Kings of Manipuri played polo in their palace gardens on these sharp, swift, strong ponies. British tea planters took up the game, and soon it was being played all over the world.

5 RIWOCHE

The Riwoche (pronounced *ree-WOE-chay*) is a small pony with tiny *duck-bill* nostrils, worked by the Bonpo people of Tibet. The Riwoche looks similar to the Przewalski's horse, although they are not related. It was unknown to the rest of the world until 1995, when a French explorer visited its home in Tibet.

6 NANGCHEN

This rare purebred horse lives high in the Tibetan mountains. As well as being nimble, the Nangchen's heart and lungs are twice the size of a normal horse's, helping it cope with the thin mountain air.

7 FERGHANA

The Ferghana horse, now extinct, was so beautiful, imposing, and fast that Emperor Wu of Han China named it the heavenly horse and even fought a war over it. The Ferghana was also called *Soulon*, meaning vegetarian dragon, due to the bony knobs on its forehead.

INDIA

DID YOU KNOW?

The Kathiawari and Marwari horses have unique lyre-shaped ears that can turn 180 degrees, picking up even the slightest sound.

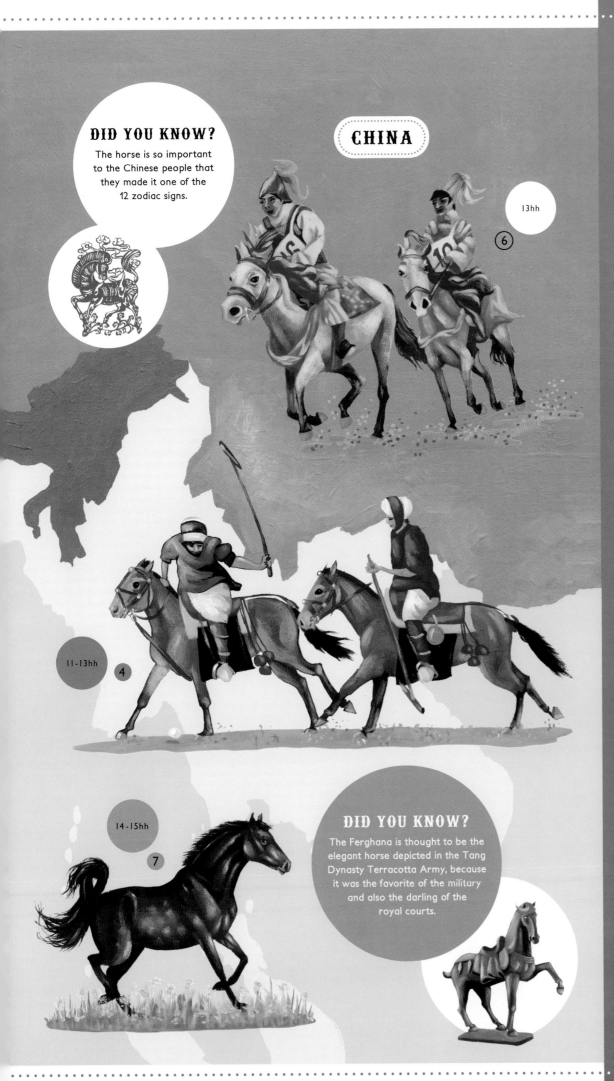

DID YOU KNOW?

The horse is so important to the Chinese people that they made it one of the 12 zodiac signs.

13hh

⑥

11-13hh ④

14-15hh

⑦

DID YOU KNOW?

The Ferghana is thought to be the elegant horse depicted in the Tang Dynasty Terracotta Army, because it was the favorite of the military and also the darling of the royal courts.

India's elegant, loyal, and adaptable horses possess incredible stamina. They have served their owners' countries in many fantastic ways, including being frequent guests of honor at weddings and acting as regal bearers of the groom.

More than 2,000 years ago, Ma Yuan, general of the Chinese army and horse expert, declared, "Horses are the foundation of military power, the great resource of the state; but, should this falter, the state will fall."

29

2 10-12hh

1

2

3 11.2-12.2hh

3

AUSTRALIA

14-16.2hh

6

1 JAVA

Tireless and willing, this tiny pony pulls carts as the local taxi service for the islands.

2 TIMOR

Tough and enthusiastic, this clever pony used to work in the circuses that traveled around Australia.

3 SUMBA

When the nyale sea worm swims to shore, it's time for the Pasola Festival in Sumba. *Pasola* (which means spear) is a jousting competition that celebrates the beginning of rice planting season.

4 BRUMBY

When machinery took over farming and industrial tasks, many horses escaped, and became the Brumby's ancestors. The Brumby is named after the farrier James Brumby. They roam in mobs in the Australian Alps. They are intelligent and easily trained when caught, making perfect riding horses.

5 WALER

Large and big boned, the Waler was thought to be the finest cavalry horse in the world. Over 130,000 Walers accompanied the Cavalry to fight in World War 1. To commemorate their contributions, one horse named Sandy (who served with the fallen Major General Sir Wiliam Bridges) returned home.

6 AUSTRALIAN STOCK HORSE

Bred from a mix of Iberian, Thoroughbred, Welsh, and Timor ponies, this strong, smart, quick horse was essential in developing farming in Australia.

DID YOU KNOW?

Esther Martha Stace was a fearless and graceful Australian horsewoman. She often took part in dingo hunts around the mountains and scrub of Yarrowitch, and she made her horse riding debut at the Walcha Show in 1891. In 1915, Esther set the world sidesaddle record by clearing a 6.6 foot jump with the horse Emu Plains. This record remained unbroken for 98 years!

1 11.2-12hh

DID YOU KNOW?
At the annual Kuda Renggong in Western Java, horses move to the rhythm of the drums while wearing vibrantly colored costumes. During this festival these agile horses dance with local performance artists. Now that's a party animal!

4 13-16.2hh

5

6

5 15-16hh

Despite being home to so many interesting creatures, Australia had no horses at all until 1788, when the First Fleet arrived from England. It is said that modern Australia was forged on the back of a horse, because within a few decades, almost every other person in Australia had a horse.

Most Indonesian ponies are a mixture of Mongolian and oriental horses. They are obliging and adaptable. Each breed has developed to suit the local needs of the island they inhabit.

PULLING CARTS

The Gypsy Vanner (13-16hh) is part of a Traveler's family. The Vanner is gentle, yet strong enough to pull the beautifully decorated *vardo* (wagon). Vanners are trained not to stop when traveling uphill. Why? They might not be able to restart!

EXPLORATION

Siberian and Icelandic horses were used in polar explorations in the early 1900s. These little horses could cope with temperatures of -58 degrees Fahrenheit and pull sleighs weighing around 1,202 pounds. There was one problem—there is no grass in the Arctic! Fortunately, the horses were happy to eat hay, dog biscuits—and even meat! The last equestrian polar expedition was led by German scientist Alfred Wegener in 1930.

POLICE

Flags, flares, fires, beating drums, tennis balls hurled at force, and even exploding petrol bombs are all part of a police horse's riot training.

The Royal Canadian Mounted Police's (*Mounties*) world-famous Musical Ride troop entertains crowds all over Canada, demonstrating the skills of both the horses and their riders. Originally, however, the ride was part of the cavalry's drill routine.

CAVALRY

Most of the handsome black horses of the British Household Cavalry are taken from Irish stock. As a reward for taking their state ceremonial duties seriously, they are taken to the coast on a two week holiday every year.

FARMING

The stock horse has cow sense, making it easier for the horse and rider to herd cattle in the right direction.

Before the invention of tractors, heavy horses, such as the Shire, were indispensable on the farm. Today, the Shire is a rare breed, but you can still watch these gentle giants in plowing competitions.

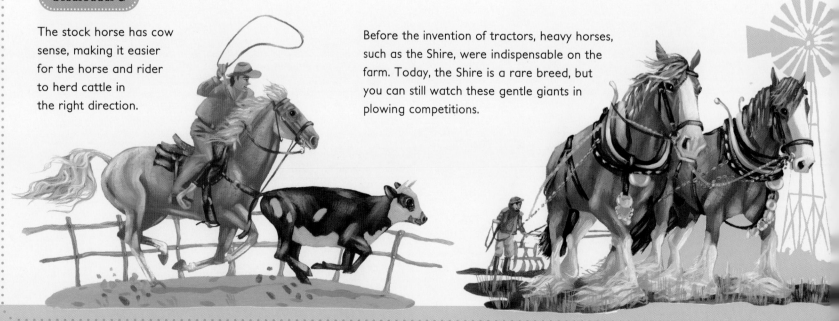

FUNERAL CARRIAGES

On some occasions, a horse drawn funeral carriage may be used. This requires horses with good manners and grace, such as these two Friesian horses.

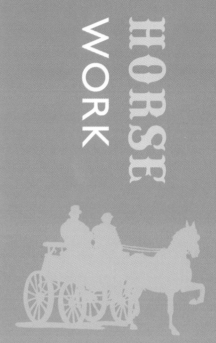

COLONIZATION

The Narragansett Pacer was first bred by settlers in North America. It gave an extremely comfortable ride and was exceptionally fast. However, this small, spirited, and surefooted horse also coped well in hot climates. The Narragansett was soon popular in the West Indies where it worked with the slaves on the sugar plantations. But mysteriously, by the early 1800s, this wonderful little horse was extinct. No one is entirely sure how that happened.

Four inventions have helped humans get the most out of their horses. First, more than 6,000 years ago, the harness was created in China. With this the horse could be controlled and trained.

A thousand years later, in Iraq, the Sumerians invented the wheel. Horse-drawn vehicles made it easier to plow, transport crops, goods, building materials, and people.

Around 700 BCE in Persia, the Scythians were the first people to sit astride their horses. It wasn't that comfortable, so they invented the saddle.

The iron stirrup was invented in China around 400 CE. This gave the rider better balance and weapons could now be used with greater accuracy.

The invention of the steam engine, or Iron Horse, in the 18th century meant that humans became much less dependent on horses for work.

FILM

Filmmakers often want beautiful horses with a strong screen presence and an incredibly patient nature. Many actors have had little experience in the saddle. Starring in many films, such as *Gladiator* and *Robin Hood*, Rusty is the perfect horse for even the most nervous rider.

Here he is in character and costume in *Snow White and the Hunter*.

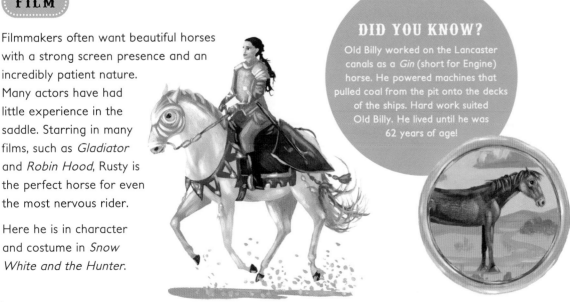

DID YOU KNOW?

Old Billy worked on the Lancaster canals as a *Gin* (short for Engine) horse. He powered machines that pulled coal from the pit onto the decks of the ships. Hard work suited Old Billy. He lived until he was 62 years of age!

DRESSAGE

Sir Lee Pearson CBE is a British Paralympic athlete. He has won more than 30 gold medals in international class dressage. These include 11 Olympic gold medals. Many of these were won on his warmblood Zion.

SHOW JUMPING

Boundaries were introduced to the English countryside following the Enclosure Acts of 1773, so foxhunters needed horses that could jump fences. In France, fences were placed inside arenas so spectators could watch. Originally called *lepping*, it caught on fast! By 1912, show jumping was an Olympic sport.

O-MOK-SEE

'O-Mok-See' is a Blackfeet Tribe word that means riding big dance. This was originally a pre-battle ritual, but it's now a competitive sport, testing the skills and sharp wits of both horse and rider.

GYMKHANA

At a gymkhana, young riders and their ponies must complete a series of challenges, where excellent jumping, turning, and stopping skills are needed. The agile Welsh Mountain Ponies frequently go home with first prize.

ARCHERY

Archers must aim their bow and shoot an arrow accurately at a moving target while galloping at 30 miles per hour. This requires complete harmony between rider and horse, and takes years of practice to achieve.

TEAM CHASING

In this exciting British equestrian sport, teams of four compete on a cross country course that covers 2 miles. There are approximately 25 fences to be jumped! The teams start at intervals and race against the clock to determine the winners.

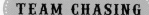

ENDURANCE

Stamina and speed are essential in endurance riding. The Tevis Cup race in the US follows the 100 mile route of the 19th century Pony Express. It covers tough terrain, including high altitudes and extreme temperatures.

DRIVING

Whether it's a gentle jaunt around a country park or splashing through muddy streams at high speed, there will be some aspect of driving that almost anyone (and almost any horse or pony) can enjoy.

RACING

With gleaming horses and jockeys in brightly colored silks thundering past at speeds nearing 40 miles per hour, you can see why horse racing has been called the Sport of Kings.

Chariot racing was probably the first mass spectator sport. In 680 BCE the Ancient Greeks built a hippodrome at Olympia for horse and chariot races. Chariot races were spectacular entertainment: fast, dangerous, and very exciting.

Horse racing is still big business now. Huge fortunes can be won in a day at events, such as the Dubai World Cup, where horses are flown in from all over the world to participate.

Working horses were trained in many skills which were also useful in battle and hunting. Today, sports horses use these skills in activities like show jumping, dressage, and cross country.

HORSEBALL

Imagine basketball on horseback, and you'll have a good idea of what horseball looks like! Ex-racehorses, when retrained, make excellent mounts for this impressive, fast, and furious sport.

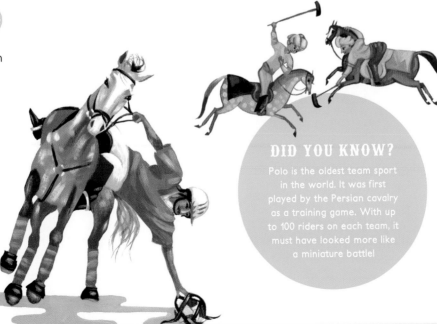

DID YOU KNOW?

Polo is the oldest team sport in the world. It was first played by the Persian cavalry as a training game. With up to 100 riders on each team, it must have looked more like a miniature battle!

ROLLING

Rolling after a bath or during a hot day is both cooling and drying. Horses will often have a favorite patch to roll in. It helps the horse shed hair. The mud and dust act as an insect repellant. Rolling can also be contagious. If one horse goes down, others may soon join in!

GROOMING

A horse's skin is thinner, with more nerve endings than human skin. This is why they prefer being scratched rather than being patted—especially on their favorite itchy spot! Horses often groom each other when they are out in the field. This act of friendship is not just about picking off burrs, it is also a soothing massage after a day's work.

COMMUNICATION

Ears are good indicators of how a horse is feeling.

- Ears to the side: listening to a rider or a noise
- Drooping ears: relaxed
- Ears pricked forward: interested
- Ears pinned back... watch out!

DID YOU KNOW?

You may think that a horse is laughing when it makes this funny face called a *flehman response*. It is made in response to an interesting, usually horsey, scent that they want to investigate.

HORSE TALK

Research suggests that horses can have up to 17 different expressions. That's three more than chimps and only ten fewer than us! They can remember a human's face from the first meeting and will respond in kind. So don't forget to smile gently when you greet a pony—you may be judged on first impressions!

HACKING

One of the best ways for a pony to experience different sights, smells, and sounds, is to *hack out* along country lanes, over fields, through woodlands and across streams. Here horse and rider can be at one with each other, developing both trust and a strong bond.

URBAN PONIES

Some riding school ponies help children, who may not have had the opportunity to connect with horses, to overcome many difficulties and gain confidence within a safe and positive environment.

The ponies teach them to engage, to be calm, and to pay attention to their needs. The children discover that with respect and patience they will win the trust of their equine friends.

BUCKING

When put out to pasture a horse may buck with the excitement of being let out of its stable and to burn off pent-up energy. Bucking is also a defense against predators—if they are being mistreated or are in pain, this may include the rider!

SLEEPING

Horses will only lie down for REM sleep when they are feeling relaxed, safe, and secure. This is the deep sleep that is essential for full revitalization. They don't lie down for long, however, as their heavy bodies put weight on their internal organs.

SPOOKING

Horses see things differently than humans. They have superior night sight and can notice the tiniest flicker of movement in their field of vision. However, they can struggle with detail, often seeing things as flat and hazy.

Sometimes objects will disappear as the horse approaches them. This is because of a blind spot directly in front of its eyes. The horse may lower its head to get a better look or jump sideways—this is called spooking.

SERVICE HORSES

Miniature horses make excellent service animals. Compared to dogs, they live much longer, and being both taller and stronger they are ideal for giving support to people with balance and mobility issues.

In 2019, Flirty made aviation history, becoming the first service horse to accompany her owner (who suffers from anxiety issues) on a plane!

THERAPY

Peyo is a horse that appears to have a remarkable ability to detect tumors and cancer, and reduce the drugs needed. Gentle and affectionate, he lessens anxiety and comforts patients in pain. He went from the dressage arena to therapy sessions, volunteering in Calais Hospital in France, where he became known as Doctor Peyo. He chooses which rooms to enter by raising his leg toward a door.

Horses are friendly and sociable animals, happiest in the company of others. They communicate using a variety of expressions and sounds, greeting their friends with a nicker and a nuzzle.

Horses prefer to avoid conflict and would much rather run away from danger or pain than fight. They are gentle creatures that usually only resort to biting or kicking when they can't escape.

Along with their sensitive nature and ability to read expressions, horses also have finely tuned hearing and a remarkable sense of smell. This means that many equines, large and small, are successful at working in various fields of therapy.

BEAUTIFUL JIM KEY

Known as the smartest horse on Earth, Beautiful Jim Key was the biggest act at the St Louis World's Fair of 1904. He could count, spell, and use the telephone, and was even trusted to go to the bank and return with the right sum of money! Jim was trained by Dr William Key, a former slave and self-taught vet, who campaigned tirelessly for the kinder treatment of animals.

GODOLPHIN ARABIAN

In 1724, Sham, meaning *sun*, was born at the Sultan's Palace in Yemen. The Sultan generously presented Sham as a gift to Louis XV of France. However, Louis thought the horse was ugly and worthless and sent him to work as a carthorse on the streets of Paris. Englishman Edward Coke, while visiting the city, saw tremendous potential in the wretched beast and bought him. Coke returned Sham to his former glory, before selling him to the 2nd Earl of Godolphin, who renamed him...Godolphin. He was one of the three Arabian stallions used to create the Thoroughbred.

SERGEANT RECKLESS

Most horses run away from danger, but Reckless ran toward it. Staff Sergeant Reckless is the only horse ever to be promoted to the rank of sergeant. She carried ammunition to the front line during the Korean War and rescued wounded soldiers. She not only shared the soldiers' tents, but also their meals, enjoying scrambled eggs and chocolate bars. In *Life* magazine's special edition celebrating heroes, she was listed alongside Martin Luther King, Mother Theresa, and Abraham Lincoln.

MISTER ED

Bamboo Harvester played Mister Ed, the famous talking horse in the 1960s US TV comedy *Mister Ed*. His trainer made him appear to talk by tickling his lips with a piece of string. The bond between trainer and horse soon became so strong that the trainer only had to touch a hoof to encourage the clever horse to move his mouth as if he was chatting.

DID YOU KNOW?

Trigger was a registered Palamino horse who starred alongside the singing cowboy, Roy Rogers in 81 films and 100 episodes of *The Roy Rogers Show*. When Trigger died, aged 33, Roy Rogers had Trigger stuffed and mounted. Trigger has since been exhibited in such places as the Texan Cowboy Hall of Fame.

BUCEPHALUS

Bucephalus was a huge black Thessalian stallion, with a reputation for being vicious and untamable. Alexander the Great was the only one who dared go near him. He turned the horse's head toward the sun as Bucephalus was afraid of his own shadow (many horses are) and the beast was instantly tamed.

We have met many different horses and ponies that have been bred to perform different tasks in various environments. There are some horses, however, that have performed incredible feats above and beyond the ones they were bred to do.

Meet a handful of horses of exceptional intelligence, stamina, courage, and character!

These unique horses have all carried out remarkable and unusual tasks, with unrivaled trust in their like-minded human partners.

They have been rewarded for their outstanding loyalty. Books have been written, films made, and statues erected to honor these superstar horses.

Here are some of their stories. Of course, some may be truer than others!

Finder's Key's career began on the racetrack, but of the four races he ran, his best result was fifth place. A canny horse whisperer reckoned Finder would perform better on screen. Like many stars, Finder is prone to throwing tantrums and having hissy fits. But, oh, how he loves the camera! And the camera loves him: Finder has starred in several films, including *Seabiscuit*, *Zorro*, and the wonderful *War Horse*.

FINDER'S KEY

MARENGO

Emperor Napoleon Bonaparte loved his horse Marengo. Incredibly brave and loyal, this small grey Arab was with the French emperor through the whole of the Napoleonic wars. He galloped from the Mediterranean Sea to Paris at the age of 19, and walked 3,000 miles to Moscow and back. His skeleton is displayed at the National Army Museum in Chelsea, England.

39

The legendary unicorn has a horse-like body, but with cloven feet and the beard of a goat. This shy, beautiful creature represents purity and grace, and is also said to be strong and fierce. The unicorn lives deep in the forests and is rarely seen. It can drink from any source because its precious horn makes poisoned water drinkable.

UNICORN

SLEIPNIR

In Norse mythology, Sleipnir (which means one who glides) was the fearless steed ridden by Odin throughout his kingdom. As grey as a thundercloud, this eight-legged horse was swifter than any other beast, on land, sea, or air. Sleipnir had the power to carry Odin to visit the Queen of the Underworld and return without so much as a blister.

FOUR HORSEMEN OF THE APOCALYPSE

These are the horses you really don't want to meet. They symbolize all the evils said to bring about the end of the world. The rider of the white horse plans to conquer everything in its path. The red horse represents the fire and bloody slaughter of war. The rider of the black horse carries scales, representing famine. Finally, the pale horse is the symbol of Death.

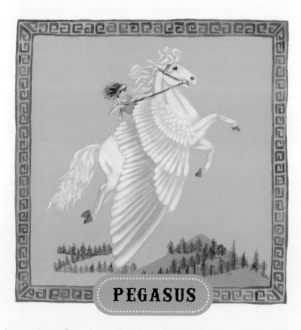

PEGASUS

In ancient Greek mythology, Pegasus, son of Poseidon, was a flying horse that helped Bellerophon, his brother, destroy the Chimera. Flying over the fire-breathing beast's head, Bellerophon poured lead into the Chimera's mouth, killing the monster. After this victory, Pegasus worked for Zeus, carrying lightning bolts. Zeus rewarded him by transforming him into the Pegasus constellation, placing him among the stars.

Celtic goddess Epona rode a white horse symbolizing beauty, purity, and fertility, and is generally pictured with horses. She was the protector of horses, donkeys, and anyone who worked with them. When someone died on horseback, she would carry their souls to the afterlife. The Romans adopted Epona, dedicating a shrine to her in nearly every stable in their empire.

EPONA

KELPIE

The shape-shifting kelpie is a Scottish water spirit. Standing beside a loch's still waters, the kelpie seems like a tame pony. But beware! It's said that any rider will become stuck to its magical coat and the kelpie will then dive into the deep waters to eat its victim. However, the stories also say that anyone who manages to catch the kelpie by its bridle will win control over a creature that has the strength of ten horses.

According to Hindu scriptures, Uchchaihshravas was the very first horse in existence and emerged from the churning milky waves of the Indian Ocean. White as the moon and bearing seven heads, this flying horse was claimed by Indra, the god-king of heaven. They became inseparable and would do anything in the world for each other.

UCHCHAIHSHRAVAS

HIPPOCAMPUS

Poseidon was the god of the sea and of earthquakes. His *hippocampi* were magnificent white horses with fish tails, who pulled his chariot across the waves. When he was angry, Poseidon was said to strike the ground with his trident, making the white horses of the sea rear up and the land to shake.

Chiron was a centaur, half-human and half-horse. He was adopted by Apollo, the Greek god of knowledge, who taught him medicine, astrology, music, and archery. Chiron became a healer, a prophet, and a teacher. One day, a drunken brawl broke out among his fellow centaurs and Chiron was killed by a poisoned arrow. Zeus rewarded him for his bravery and kindness by placing him up among the stars as the constellation Sagittarius.

CHIRON

Horses star in the myths and legends of many cultures around the world because they have played such an important role in human history. White horses were adored above all.

Cyrus the Great, a king of ancient Persia, rode white Nisean stallions. When one of his stallions drowned in the Gyndes, he is said to have drained the river. He could not believe a river would kill something so beautiful.

The ancient gods also loved white horses, which represented freedom, power, and nobility. They carried the gods through the skies, over the seas, and along mysterious underground passages.

Some mythical horses have unique features, such as horns, wings, extra legs, and heads. Some have exceptional strength. And some you just don't want to meet!

10-11hh

WALES

2

NORTH AMERICA

1

4

12.3-13.1hh

PORTUGAL

NAMIBIA

3

14.2-16hh

3

1 MUSTANG

The mustang can go from quietly grazing to stampeding across the American prairies in an instant. This is because, in the wild, horses have been threatened by predators, such as coyotes and cougars. Horses receive low-frequency sounds that travel via their teeth and jawbones to their ears. As soon as they sense danger, they will gallop off.

2 CARNEDDAU

Henry VIII of England ordered all native ponies too small to carry his knights in armor into battle, to be slaughtered. Happily, his men failed to find the Carneddau ponies, hidden away behind the craggy mountain range of Eryri (also known as Snowdonia) in North Wales. Here, they continue to live, maintaining the landscape by grazing on the gorse, and creating tracks by trampling the bracken.

3 NAMIB DESERT HORSE

This desert horse is constantly on the move, covering vast areas in search of watering holes and grazing. They live peacefully alongside each other, though occasionally a fight will break out when a young stallion tries to join the band of a dominant stallion. Even though these brief fights look dramatic, contact is rarely made. The performance is mainly for show.

4 GARRANO

The Garrano is so rare that it has become a protected species. It lives in the Peneda Gerês National Park in Portugal and shares this space with another protected species, the predatory Iberian wolf! The mares protect their foals by forming a circle around the young. The stallion will patrol the circle, ready to charge should any threat arise.

5 KONIK

The blue dun coated Koniks are excellent eco-engineers. They are employed in rewilding projects on the wetlands in England, Holland and Ukraine. Thriving on thick clumps of tough grasses and woody shoots, they leave behind piles of fertile droppings. Their water-filled hoofprints soon become pools, encouraging a diversity of flowers and grasses to grow, attracting waterfowl and bugs.

6 PRZEWALSKI'S HORSE

According to folklore, this ancient species was the mount of the gods. They were given the name *takhi*, which means spirit or worthy of worship in Mongolian. Young colts who begin to test the dominant stallion's authority are chased away from the harem and form a bachelor herd. Here they play and compete until they lead their own band.

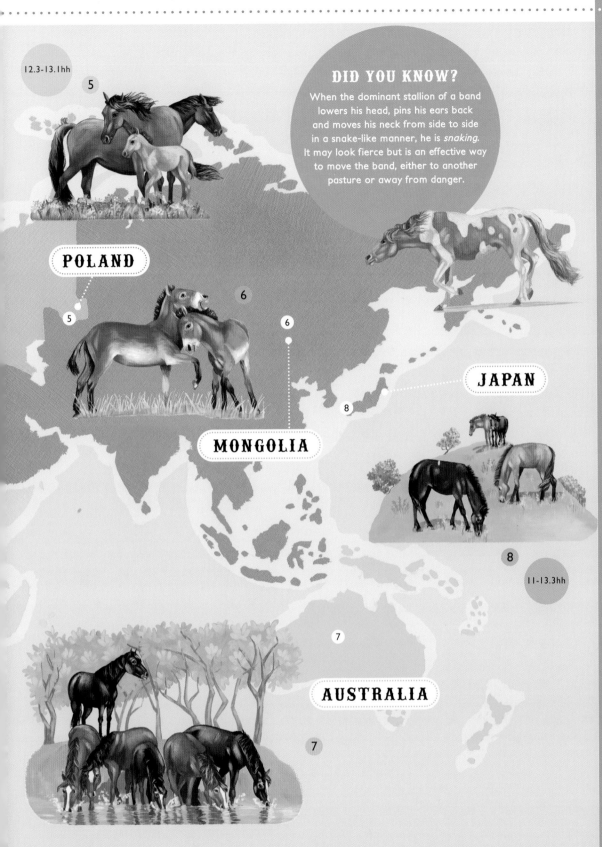

12.3-13.1hh

5

DID YOU KNOW?

When the dominant stallion of a band lowers his head, pins his ears back and moves his neck from side to side in a snake-like manner, he is *snaking*. It may look fierce but is an effective way to move the band, either to another pasture or away from danger.

POLAND

5

6

6

MONGOLIA

JAPAN

8

8

11-13.3hh

7

AUSTRALIA

7

Feral horses are free-ranging horses whose ancestors were once domesticated. They remain largely untouched by humans.

They live in large herds, which are made up of smaller groups of up to 25 horses called *harems* or *bands*. There is usually one dominant mare and stallion. The mare is often in charge of the band, leading it to water, guiding it to safety, and constantly checking on the well-being of her family.

These horses can travel up to 31 miles a day and graze for up to 18 hours. Because their appetites are simple and space is plentiful, there is little to fight over!

7 BRUMBY

Even though the Brumby can survive the rocky ranges and climate of the semi-arid deserts, they prefer the swampy marshlands of Australia's Northern Territory. Despite having no natural predators, at least one member of the herd will always remain alert to possible danger, while the others graze or have a drink in the shady streams.

8 MISAKI

The Misaki, meaning beautiful blossom, is a rare and ancient breed. In the 16th century it was made a popular warhorse. In 1953, the Misaki was named a Japanese National Natural Treasure, along with its habitat on Toimisaki (also known as Cape Toi). Here it roams freely, grazing on the pampas grass and ferns, protected against predators and poachers. Its only human onlookers now are tourists.

43

BOLTING When a horse gallops off out of control; usually due to fear

CAVALRY Army division on horseback

CLOVEN FOOT Hoof that is divided into two parts

COB Stocky and steady-natured large pony or horse

COMPETITION HORSE Horse kept and trained to compete

CONSTELLATION Configuration of stars that form a pattern

DISHED FACE Inward curved face

DRAFT HORSE Calm, strong horses adapted for pulling heavy loads

DRESSAGE Trained horses performing various precision movements

EQUUS Genus of mammals, including the horse, zebra, ass and donkey

FARRIER Person who shoes horses and is trained in equine foot care

FEATHERS Long hairs on the lower legs of some—mainly draft—horses

FERAL Undomesticated animals that live in the wild

FLAXEN MANE Lighter than body colour; usually a golden shade

FOXTROT Smooth gait between a trot and a walk

GAIT A horse's various movements at different speeds, including walking, trotting and galloping

GRADE HORSE Mixed breed horse (not a purebred), unregistered horse

HIPPODROME Oval stadium used for horse competitions or performances

HORSE WHISPERER Trainer who uses gentle, non-aggressive methods

HOUSEHOLD CAVALRY The two senior regiments of the British Army

IBERIAN HORSE Horse breeds from the Iberian peninsula, including Spain and Portugal

JOUSTING Tournament where knights or riders compete on horseback with lances

MARE Adult, female horse or other equine

NICKER Soft, low sound that is usually a friendly greeting

NOMAD Person of no fixed address who moves from place to place to find work, food, and fresh pastures for their animals

ORIENTAL HORSE Spirited, bold, hot-blooded horses well adapted to a hot dry climate

PACKHORSE Horse used to carry goods on its back or in saddlebags

REM Rapid eye movement, which happens during deep sleep

PONY EXPRESS US mail system that was operated by a relay of horses and riders

ROACHED When the mane is trimmed so short the hairs stand up straight

RODEO Competition where cowhands show off their riding skills

SIDESADDLE Special saddle for female riders where both legs are on one side

SILKS Colorful shirts and caps worn by jockeys that indicate the horse's owner

SIRE Horse's father

STALLION Adult male horse used for breeding

STOCK HORSE Agile horse used for herding cattle

THESSALIAN Ancient breed used by Roman and Greek soldiers

UNGULATE Hoofed animal, generally herbivorous

VARDO Highly decorated traditional horse-drawn wagon

WARMBLOOD Type of middle weight horse, bred to be calm and athletic for battle, farming, and equestrian events

Did you find **80** living breeds in this book?